Creative Careers

Makeup Artist

Helen Mason

Please visit our website, **www.garethstevens.com**. For a free color catalog of all our high-quality books, call toll free 1-800-542-2595 or fax 1-877-542-2596.

Library of Congress Cataloging-in-Publication Data

Mason, Helen.
Makeup artist / by Helen Mason.
p. cm. — (Creative careers)
Includes index.
ISBN 978-1-4824-1341-0 (pbk.)
ISBN 978-1-4824-1303-8 (6-pack)
ISBN 978-1-4824-1449-3 (library binding)
1. Theatrical makeup — Vocational guidance — Juvenile literature. 2. Film makeup — Vocational guidance — Juvenile literature. 3. Makeup artists — Vocational guidance. I. Mason, Helen, 1950-. II. Title.
PN2068.M37 2015
792—d23

First Edition

Published in 2015 by
Gareth Stevens Publishing
111 East 14th Street, Suite 349
New York, NY 10003

Developed and produced for Gareth Stevens Publishing by BlueApple*Works* Inc.
Editor: Marcia Abramson
Art Director: Melissa McClellan
Designer: Joshua Avramson

Photo Credits: Corbis: Louis Burgis p. 41 bottom;Dreamstime: © Photosdl p. 4; © Robert Lerich p. 8 top; © Ipb p. 8 bottom; © Marina Pissarova p. 9 top; © Rui Matos p. 12; © Mira Agron p. 13 right; © Pindiyath100 p. 18; © Dikiiy p. 22; © Triciadaniel p. 23; © Edward Fielding p. 24 bottom; © Catzovescu p. 28; © Gordana Sermek p. 30 top; © Costin79 p. 30; © Monkey Business Images p. 34; © Anton Oparin p. 37; © Sbukley p. 40 top; © Darko64 p. 44 top; © Wangkun Jia p. 44; iStock: © roey p.14; © RuslanDashinsky p. 18 top; © rollover p. 19; © microgen p. 31; © Asian p. 35; © CEFutcher p. 45; © John Chapple p. 36; Keystone Press: © Steve Kosko p. 9; Photofest: Revolution/Columbia; Public Domain: p. 40 bottom; p. 42 top; Shutterstock: © Piotr Marcinski cover; © NemesisINC cover top left; © Vorobyeva cover top right; © Wallenrock cover bottom left; © Seprimor cover bottom right; © Paul Tarasenko title p.; © Africa Studio TOC background; © jesadaphorn yellow note paper; © Flashon Studio TOC; © Anton Oparin p. 5; © Roman Sinichkin p. 7; © Thor Jorgen Udvang p. 10 top; © Korionov p.10 bottom; © Axel Lauer p. 11 left; © Helga Esteb p. 11 right; © Anton Oparin p. 16; © bikeriderlondon p. 17; © Deborah Kolb p. 20; © Blend Images p. 21; © sherwood p. 24 top; © Dikiiy p. 26; © Anton Oparin p. 27; © Icons Jewelry p. 29; © Pinkcandy p. 32; © Jeff Cameron Collingwood p. 33; © luminaimages p. 38; © Igor Bulgarin p. 39; © lev radin p. 41 top; © leoks p. 42; © Sergei Bachlakov p. 43; SuperStock: imagebroker.net; Thinkstock: © Fuse p. 6; © Tanya Constantine p. 28 top; U.S. Air Force photo: Tech. Sgt. Larry A. Simmons p. 13 left; Wikkicommons: © Derrick Tyson p. 14 top

Manufactured in the United States of America

CPSIA compliance information: Batch #CS15GS. For further information contact Gareth Stevens, New York, New York at 1-800-542-2595.

Contents

What Is a Makeup Artist?

Makeup artists are professional artists who use their skills to change or improve people's looks. They work with sponges, makeup brushes, and makeup to make a person look a certain way.

Enhancing Appearance

Many jobs require that people look attractive because they work in front of cameras or a TV show audience, in a movie, on a stage, on a runway, or appear in photographs. A makeup artist fixes these people's appearance prior to their performance to achieve the right effect with the lighting and to help them look their best while performing.

◀ *All models and actors use makeup artists to help with their looks.*

Other Jobs

Makeup artists also work on hair. This can include making someone with a lot of hair appear bald or adding a beard.

In addition, they make **prosthetics**, or artificial body parts. For example, they may make a twisted nose for an actor who is playing the part of someone with a broken nose.

Seasoned makeup artists share their knowledge with the public by working with beauty magazines as writers and editors. Many of these experts also share their makeup tips through blog posts and books and by serving on discussion panels.

Did You Know?

The use of light and dark makeup can emphasize some features and minimize others. For example, adding light makeup to the top of a nose makes it appear larger and wider.

▼ *Makeup artists use mascara, brushes, and makeup to* ***enhance*** *people's appearance.*

What Makeup Artists Do

Makeup artists work in two distinct industries. One is cosmetic and fashion and the other is theater and film. Cosmetic and fashion makeup artists work with a variety of people, from customers at a makeup counter to models. Theater and film makeup artists work with actors and actresses to bring **characters** to life on stage and in film.

Cosmetic Makeup

Aesthetics is the study of helping people look their best. Cosmetic makeup artists analyze the strengths and weaknesses of a person's appearance. They then plan how to emphasize good features and minimize others.

Some cosmetic makeup artists work with people who have birthmarks or health issues. They show people how to hide a scar or burn. They can also make eyebrows for someone who has lost them.

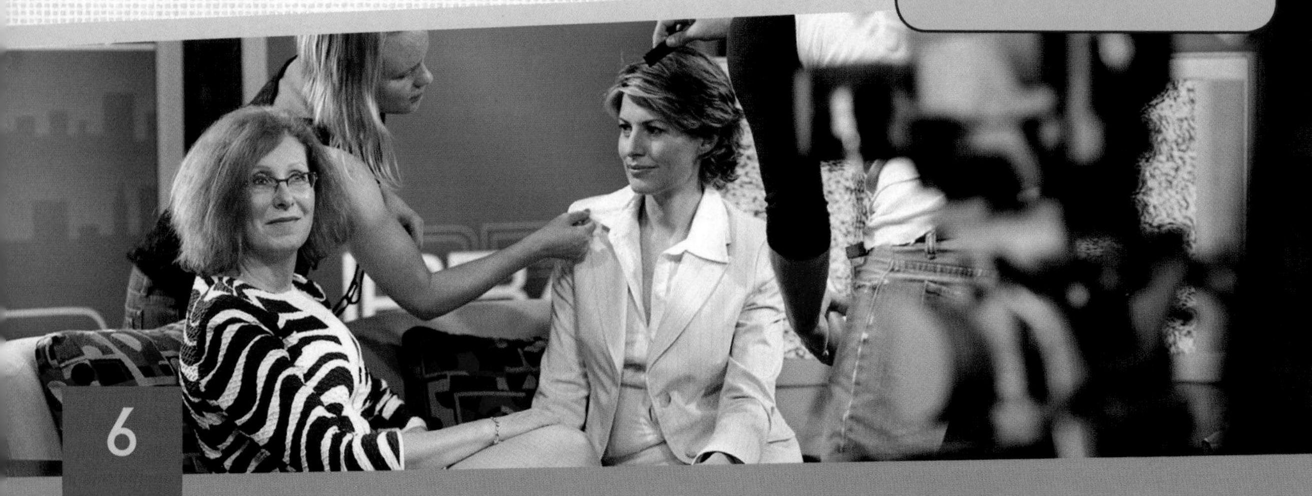

▼ *Makeup artists work on TV and film sets.*

Fashion Makeup

Fashion makeup artists prepare models for their turn on the catwalk, or runway. They provide touch-ups just before the models go on stage and may make quick makeup adjustments between appearances.

These artists also prepare models to be photographed for magazine covers and features.

Did You Know?

*Some makeup artists work with **dermatologists** and **plastic surgeons**. They can provide advice on using makeup to conceal ongoing skin treatments. They can also enhance the results of plastic surgery.*

Makeup for Theater, Film, and Television

Makeup artists for theater, film, and TV focus on actors. They study scripts and plan makeup with the needs of the character and the audience in mind. They help actors look like the character they are portraying. This can include changing a young actor into an old man or making a beautiful actress look like a witch.

▼ *A makeup artist prepares this actor to appear on stage.*

Theater and Stage Makeup

Theater and stage makeup must enhance the character being played. It must show the character's age, physical appearance, and emotional state. Depending on the story, makeup may need to show the passage of time. There are four basic types of theater and stage makeup: straight, character, stylized, and fantastic.

▲ *Straight makeup allows an actor to look like an ordinary person.*

▼ *Character makeup makes a statement about the character. It may show her as older, fatter, thinner, threatening, or devilish.*

The Character

Good makeup allows the audience to see and become involved with characters.

Proper makeup aplied by an experienced makeup artist works so well that some actors say they feel they become the character as they put on their makeup.

Lights and Audience

Stage productions use strong lights, which sometimes create shadows that affect the appearance of actors. Makeup artists must consider these shadows when applying makeup.

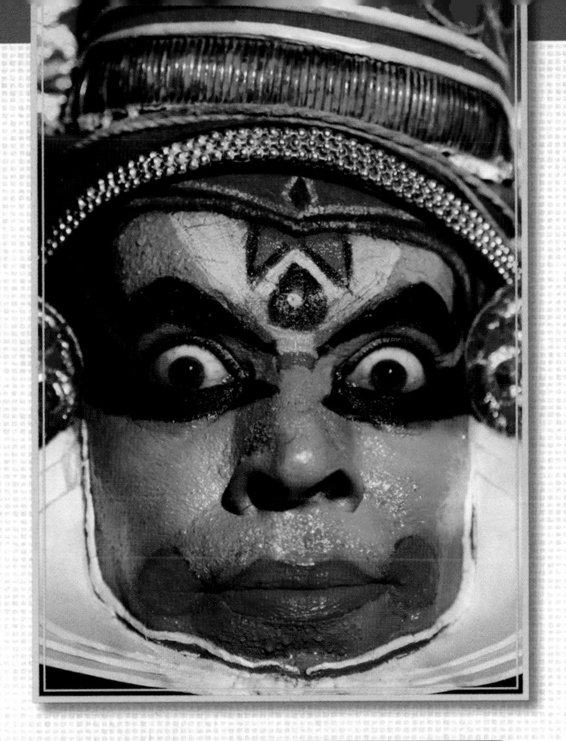

▲ *Fantastic makeup is common in ballet and opera productions.*

A lot of stage lighting is from overhead. Sit in a dark room and shine a light down onto your face. Notice the shadows it creates. Stage makeup uses light colors to enhance the areas in shadow.

Theater makeup also has to consider the audience. People in the back row need to see the characters' expressions. Strong makeup colors and the use of wigs and false beards allow this by emphasizing the color and form of the face.

◀ *This Townsend Opera performance of* The Mikado *is using stylized makeup.*

Stylized and Fantastic Stage Makeup

Makeup artists require many skill sets to create the right effect, but sometimes they become experts with a specific type of makeup, such as stylized makeup, which follows set instructions. Another example is fantastic makeup, which makes the person look completely different, even alien.

▲ *This Kabuki actor wears typical face, lip, and eyebrow makeup.*

Stylized Makeup

Japanese Kabuki theater dates back to the 1600s. All of the actors are men. Men play the parts of warriors and thieves, as well as female roles. An actor's makeup tells the audience about his gender and character.

The Kabuki actor's skin is covered with oil and then smeared with white cream. Eyebrows are painted on higher than they are naturally. The eyes are outlined in different colors. Red suggests a woman, while black is used for men.

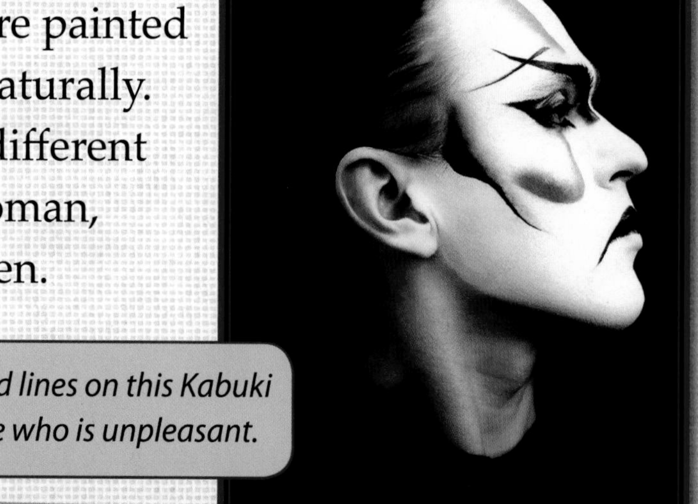

▶ *The makeup color and lines on this Kabuki villain suggest someone who is unpleasant.*

Fantastic Makeup

Fantastic makeup and special effects makeup used for movies are similar to theater makeup. Someone wearing fantastic makeup might look like a Russian wooden doll, a robot, or Frankenstein.

Frankenstein's makeup includes a **bald cap** that covers the actor's hair. Material added to the bald cap provides a bulging forehead. The nose is made larger and the chin is made square by attaching putty. Finally, makeup is applied to conceal the areas between glued-on material and real skin, and to add color to the fake skin.

Did You Know?

Kabuki makeup is so interesting that actors often pressed a cloth to their face to make a print of it. These prints were sold as souvenirs.

▼ *Creating full Frankenstein makeup demands time, teamwork, and patience.*

◀ *If needed, fantastic makeup artists can make stage actors look like living statues.*

Television and Film Makeup

Everyone who appears on television and in films wears makeup. This includes sports celebrities, TV reporters, politicians, and actors.

▲ *Makeup on news, weather, and sports announcers reduces the effect of harsh television lights.*

Television

Television lights are strong. They can pick up even the tiniest flaw in someone's makeup. Most people need just enough to make them look natural, but refreshed. This might include **concealer** to remove the circles under their eyes and to even out skin tones.

Actors may require more makeup depending on their role. It's important to use the right colors. Too much orange or blue does not look good. Some makeup artists advise against lip gloss, which can attract television lights.

Television lights also shine on oily skin. Makeup artists apply **translucent** powder that allows some light to pass through. They may also blot an actor's natural oils with tissue or rice paper.

Film

Imagine seeing your face enlarged one hundred times. Every uneven skin tone, blemish, and flaw is clear. Film actors need a makeup artist to make them look perfect.

An actor's skin needs to look the same throughout an entire scene. To stay looking fresh, performers use makeup artists to touch up their makeup between takes. Sometimes they use photos to keep the makeup consistent.

Did You Know?

Standard fluorescent light tends to be low in red light and high in green. This gives people filmed under these lights a greenish skin tone. Applying makeup with few green tones counteracts this.

▲ *A makeup artist applying makeup on actress Debra Messing while filming the TV show* Smash *in Times Square, New York City.*

▲ *Makeup artists apply makeup to everyone who appears in front of a camera—even the extras.*

Special Effects Makeup

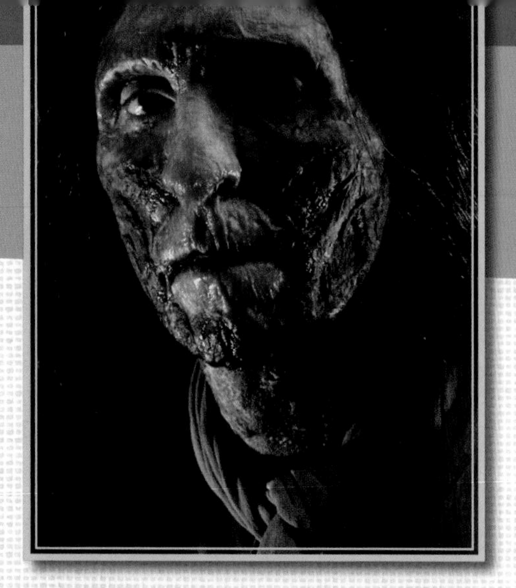

▲ *Silica was used to produce the skin of this actor playing a monster.*

Special effects makeup requires creativity and imagination. Performers need to be transformed into fictional characters, or may have to appear inhuman or even fatally wounded. Special effects makeup artists sometimes struggle to get a break in this competitive industry, but it's well worth the effort when they do succeed because the work is profitable and rewarding. This makeup includes casting an actor's face or other body part, making a mold, and then developing a prosthetic.

▼ *This actor's ears were made by first casting the actor's actual ears.*

Making the Mold

Lifecasting involves making a three-dimensional copy of all or part of someone's body. First, the body part is covered with a protective coating, such as petroleum jelly. The body part is then covered with a molding compound, such as **silicone rubber**. The material is allowed to harden and then is carefully removed.

> **Did You Know?**
>
> *Makeup artists made six wigs and eight beards for each dwarf in* The Lord of the Rings. *Each wig was made from yak hair.*

To make a copy of the body part, the mold is filled with **plaster of Paris**. The plaster is allowed to dry and the mold is removed. This cast is an exact duplicate of the body part.

Making and Applying the Prosthetic

The new body part is sculpted on top of the cast. A mold is made of this new body part. Finally, foam **latex**, gelatin, or silicone is used to make the prosthetic. This is glued to the actor's body, covering the original part.

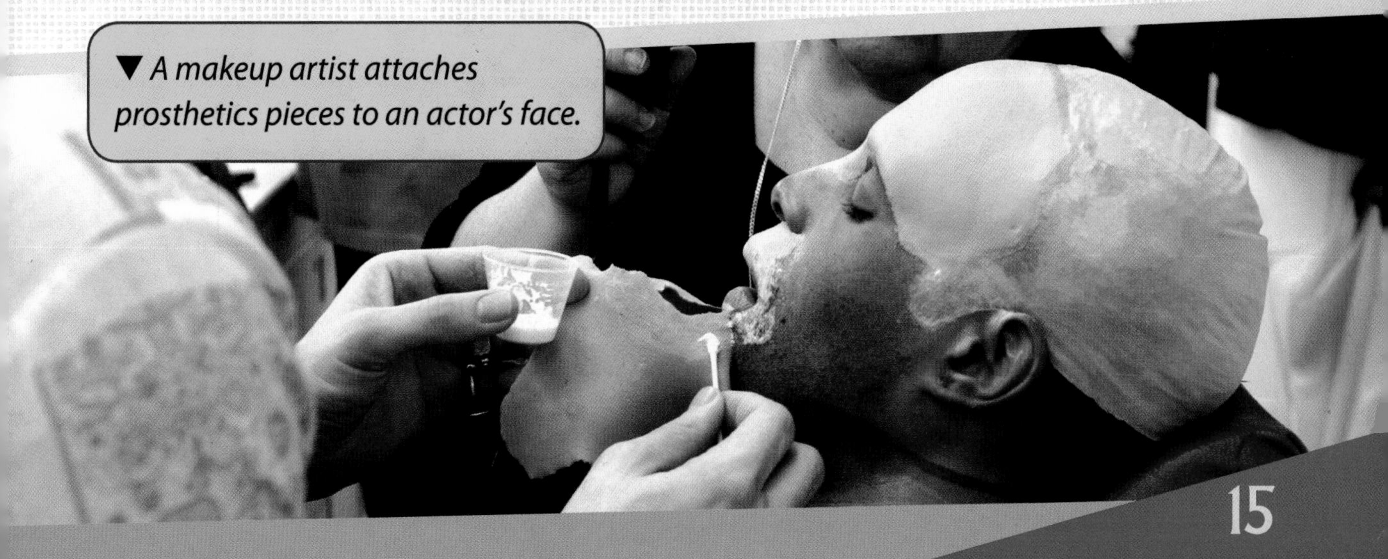

▼ *A makeup artist attaches prosthetics pieces to an actor's face.*

Fashion Shows and Photo Sessions

Fashion makeup appears in books, magazines, catalogues, and at fashion shows.

Fashion Shows

Makeup artists start planning several months before a fashion show. They meet with designers and listen to their thoughts about the fashions. Then they create makeup looks to complement these ideas.

On the day of the show, the makeup team may start as early as 4:00 a.m. to have models ready for a 10:00 a.m. opening. If there's more than one show, they run to the next location, where there are other models in need of makeup. Backstage at a fashion show can be a hectic place. A makeup artist must be able to focus and work in this atmosphere.

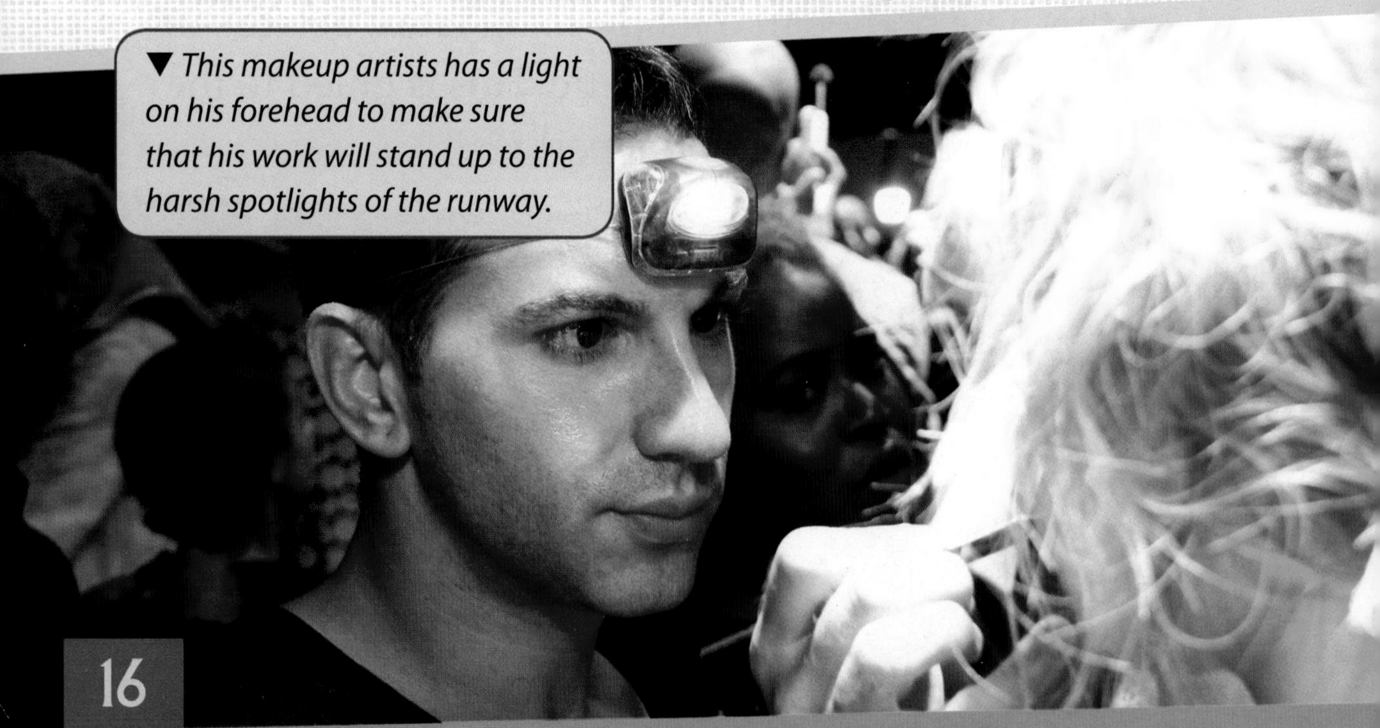

▼ *This makeup artists has a light on his forehead to make sure that his work will stand up to the harsh spotlights of the runway.*

Photo Sessions

Makeup artists use their knowledge of how the camera works to help models appear their best. Photo session makeup is subtle and uses flat colors that will not reflect the light from camera flashes.

Markup artists carefully blend in lines between the different makeup areas. They also apply darker mascara that gives a better contrast in photos. In addition, they apply powders with a yellow tint that reflects less light, thus emphasizing the beauty of the model's skin. They may also observe how a model holds her face toward the camera, and add light makeup to areas cast in shadow.

▼ *Makeup artists have to be ready to step in and make adjustments during the photo shoot.*

Selling Cosmetics

Many makeup artists get their start selling cosmetics at the beauty counter of a local store.

Corrective Makeup

Makeup sales includes giving advice about corrective makeup. This involves helping people emphasize their good points and take attention away from the bad ones.

▲ *A makeup salesperson must be be able to give advice to customers about which makeup will work best for them.*

Makeup artists understand that dark areas recede and light areas come forward. Using that knowledge and different shades of makeup, they can help someone narrow a wide forehead by applying darker makeup near the hairline. They can shade a jawline to make a chin appear pointed and add a shadow to the inner corner of the eyes to make them appear sunken.

◀ *Salespeople may offer a free sample or demonstration of a new product.*

Selling Takes Work

Cosmetics sales requires a makeup artist to listen, have a working knowledge of many types of makeup, and be confident enough to give makeup tips and make suggestions. Good salespeople are also flexible. They research the latest trends. They counsel customers on skin care. They analyze skin tones and suggest makeup shades that will enhance those tones. They also teach customers how to apply makeup.

Did You Know?

To encourage sales, makeup counters are placed near the front and center of many stores.

Most salespeople show teens how to cover blemishes and counsel brides on the latest wedding styles. Working as a makeup artist also requires people skills, such as patience, empathy, and tact, so that **clients** feel comfortable with the consultant in their personal space.

▼ *Look at the difference makeup can make. Makeup artists use sample makeovers like these as a selling tool.*

Working for Yourself

A makeup artist is considered a specialist and can be hired to do makeup for weddings and special occasions. Working in this way for many different clients is called freelancing. Freelancers are hired and paid by the job.

Advantages and Disadvantages

Freelancers work for a number of clients. They get a variety of experiences. They are paid to travel, often to exotic places, and to meet interesting and exciting people. As their expertise increases, they can charge more for their time. They are responsible for everything from finding work to accounting. It's important for a freelancer to have a positive attitude about working long hours and to have lots of good ideas about growing their business.

▼ *Many freelance makeup artists specialize in helping brides look their best.*

Variety of Work

Many freelancers work with private clients, on fashion shows, and in theater or film. They help people prepare for special events. Some offer training in how to apply makeup.

Performers are not the only people who hire makeup artists. Sometimes politicians hire a personal makeup artist for television appearances and speeches, and they also may bring them along when they travel.

Did You Know?

Shared makeup brushes and applicators can spread skin bacteria and rashes. To avoid this, makeup artists should clean makeup brushes with rubbing alcohol between clients and use disposable sponges, cotton balls, and cotton swabs.

▼ *A makeup artist prepares her client to appear at a special event.*

Related Careers

▲ *These women learn about makeup through a store event. Makeup artists help plan and work at such events.*

There are many careers related to makeup artistry. Most makeup artists work in large cities because that's where the majority of jobs are located.

Makeup Companies

Some makeup artists work for makeup companies. They train salespeople in stores how to sell their company's makeup to customers. They also plan store events that attract customers to learn about and buy a certain type of makeup. Others develop their own makeup line. They may also develop new ways to sell their products.

Image Consultants

People with good color sense and an eye for design can become image consultants. They interview clients about their needs, discuss preferences in style and color, and analyze the client's body type. They take the client on a shopping trip. Sometimes, they put together an entire wardrobe, including casual and formal wear, accessories, and makeup.

Other Careers

A tattoo is a special art form that is permanently applied to a person's skin. The art is created by a tattoo artist. This type of art is not new. People have gotten tattoos throughout history.

Face painters work at parties and other events. Many work part-time; others develop full-time businesses.

With special training in cosmetology or mortuary science, a makeup artist can work in a funeral home. At a funeral home, the makeup artist prepares the appearance of a deceased person to be viewed at their funeral. They usually work from a photo of the person.

Did You Know?

Makeup artists' incomes vary depending on their location, experience, specialization, and ability to sell themselves. The range is anywhere from $20,000 a year to over $100,000 a year.

▼ *Many face painters work at fairs, amusement parks, and arcades.*

Day in the Life of a Makeup Artist

▲ *It takes a lot of skill to make an actor look like this.*

Makeup artists use people as their canvases, and the work is fast-paced and varied. A special effects makeup artist can transform one person into an animal in the morning and another person into a terrifying creature in the afternoon. The possibilities are endless for these artists. They make a living bringing fantasy to life, and the job is both exciting and satisfying.

Getting Ready

To work as a makeup artist, a person must be punctual and detail oriented because the clients need their hair and makeup done within a certain time frame and in a specific way. It's important for the makeup artist to remember and bring all the tools needed for the day. Forgetting the necessary equipment could prevent the person from doing the job properly.

▲ *This is how a makeup artist made up an extra for a zombie movie.*

In Action

The director may give instructions for creating a certain look. Sometimes that look must be re-created for several days in a row. In that case, photographs and notes are taken to ensure that the makeup and hair are the same each day.

In special effects, makeup artists usually have the freedom to get carried away with their creations, but depending on the complexity of the design, creating a look can take many hours. Molds and casts may need to be formed prior to even starting makeup application. Wigs and fake body parts are often brought into the process. This type of work is more creative compared to typical makeup application. Special effects makeup artists work long days and don't leave until the job is finished. The next day, they do it all again.

▼ *Applying makeup correctly takes concentration, as shown here.*

The Work

▲ *Makeup artists prepare their workstations and keep the area neat and clean.*

Makeup artists are specialists who focus on only makeup. This is different than a beautician or a cosmetologist, who focuses on nail and hair care in addition to makeup. Makeup artists can work alone or as part of a team.

Preparation

The Tools—Makeup artists often purchase superior supplies and materials, so they want to take good care of these expensive items. They keep their tools organized and clean, and they also sanitize their brushes and other instruments regularly so germs are not transferred from client to client.

The Client—Prior to working together, a makeup artist consults with the client to find out about their makeup needs. Every client's expectations are different, depending on the event for which the makeup is needed. The client could be getting married, directing a musical, preparing a fashion show, or organizing a photo shoot. Once all of the questions have been answered, the work can get underway.

Taking Care of Clients

The Makeup—Each makeup application is customized to the client. First, the client's skin is cleaned with products made for their particular skin type. Next, foundations, concealers, and powders are applied. Finally, eyeliners, eyeshadows, blushes, lip liners, and lipsticks are applied. Each of these products is made for the client's skin type and is used only if the client wants it applied. When the makeup is completed, the client should look and feel spectacular as well as self-confident.

The Touchups—The makeup artist's job is not done if the client is in a play, musical, movie, or television show. The client's makeup will need to be maintained between takes. This type of makeup artistry makes for a long day.

▼ ***Airbrushing*** *makes it look as though someone has an even, natural tan.*

Makeup Tools

Makeup artists have a number of tools that help them produce great results.

Brushes

Makeup artists have a collection of quality brushes, many of them handmade. The heads are different sizes and shapes, depending on the type of brush and how it's used.

▲ *Many makeup mirrors include several lights to give the makeup artist a clear view of their* ***palette***—*which is, in this case, the face being made up.*

Airbrushes spray makeup onto the skin. They produce flawless makeup with even tones. The makeup lasts longer and can handle heat better.

Many makeup artists carry their brushes in a special brush belt when they're working.

▼*A brush belt keeps a large number of makeup brushes handy for easy use.*

Face Charts

Makeup artists use face charts to plan a new look. Makeup artists also study face charts to learn how others have achieved certain looks. The face charts are made of a special paper to which the artist can apply makeup. Unlike standard paper, this special product was made to withstand makeup applications. It can hold creams and powders quite well without being ruined. Related notes keep track of the products and colors used.

Makeup artists use these notes to maintain consistency during theatrical productions. But they are also handy for makeup artists who are new to the industry. It allows them to practice their craft while demonstrating their talents and abilities.

Did You Know?

Airbrushing was first used in 1925 in the movie Ben Hur. *It was developed to help makeup artists apply makeup to the face and body of a large number of actors.*

▼ *Face charts allow makeup artists to experiment with new looks. They can also be used to teach someone how to apply a certain look.*

EYES

Base/Primer ______________________
Brows ______________________
Eyelid ______________________
Crease ______________________
Highlight/Contour ______________________
Mascara ______________________

LIPS

Building a Makeup Kit

A basic makeup kit provides everything a makeup artist needs to get started.

Basic Makeup Kit

Makeup kits start with a container. Wheeled ones are easier to move. The inside should have a number of compartments to store makeup.

▲ *A professional makeup kit includes everything a makeup artist needs for a particular job.*

Basic contents include wipes, cleansing oil, and face **primer**. Makeup is placed in a number of palettes, one for each type of makeup. Rather than carry every possible color, makeup artists mix new ones from the colors they have.

They also carry a number of makeup-setting sprays. This is similar to hair spray, but it's for makeup. Brushes, pencils, tweezers, and safety scissors complete the basics.

▼ *Artists have different palettes for eyes, foundation, and lips.*

Other Materials

Working in special effects requires more than the standard everyday makeup. Special effects makeup artists create unique (and often strange) fantasy characters who don't exist in the real world. Creating these distinct creatures requires special materials.

Many special effects makeup artists use liquid latex, sculpting wax, various adhesives, and fake blood. These materials can be used to fake injuries or make a human look like a werewolf. **Spirit gum** or some other adhesive is used to glue the wax in place. Makeup blends it in with regular skin.

Did You Know?

Pointed cotton swabs are must-haves for most makeup artists. The pointed tip erases smudges, touches up makeup, cleans up tears, and blends colors. When dipped into makeup remover, it can also erase a problem.

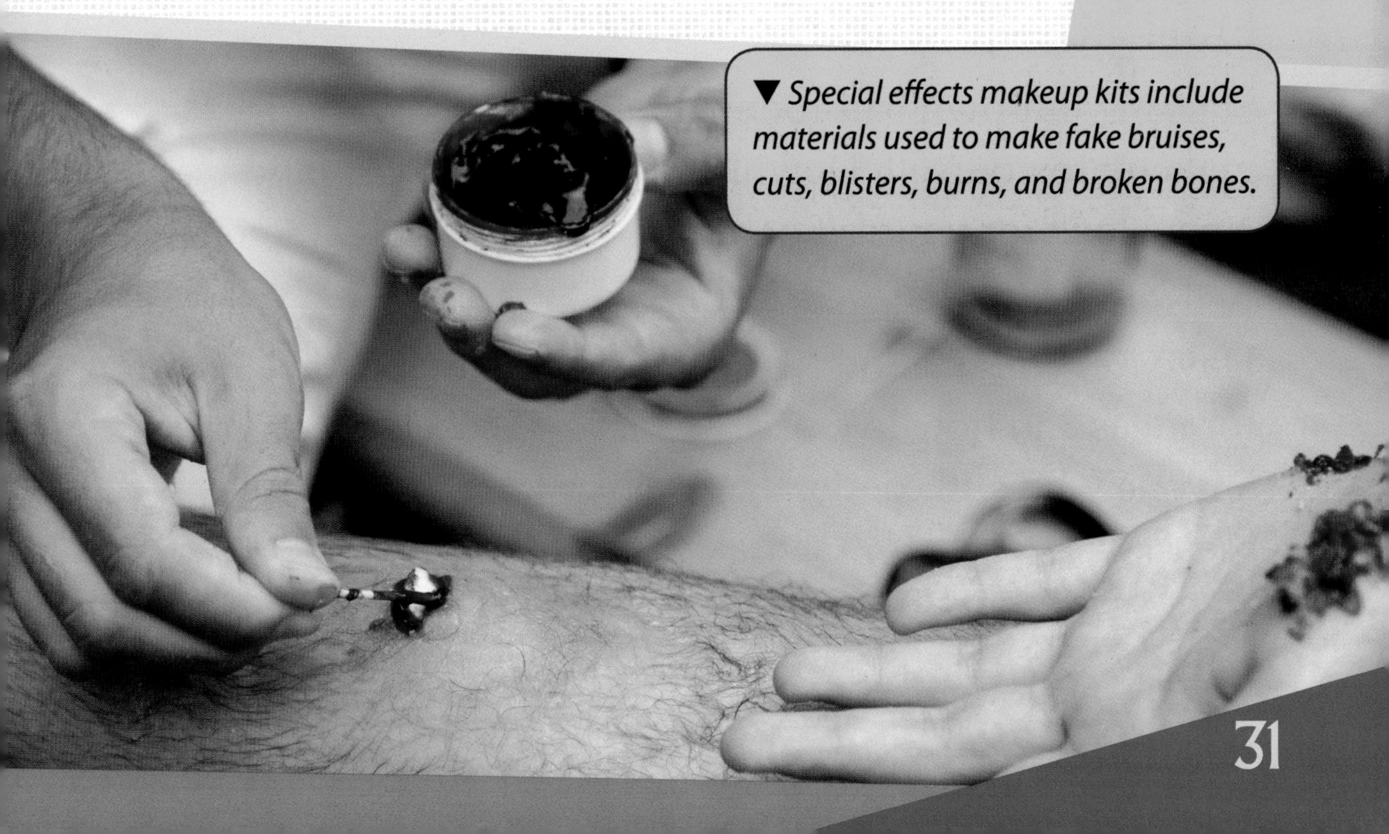

▼ *Special effects makeup kits include materials used to make fake bruises, cuts, blisters, burns, and broken bones.*

Getting Experience

▲ *Practice techniques by applying makeup on yourself. See how many different looks you can create.*

Interested in becoming a makeup artist? If you are passionate about makeup application and artistry, a career as a makeup artist might be the path to take. Experimenting and playing with makeup to create various looks is a great place to get started. Friends and family are the best clients for a budding makeup artist.

Start at Home

Start in your own bathroom or bedroom by applying makeup to yourself. Download blank face charts and plan a new look for yourself or a friend. Invite family members. Make them up, too.

Have fun with Halloween makeup. Research online for ideas and how to create them. Use special effects on anyone who will cooperate. Some artists even practice on their pets!

Other Places

Offer to help do makeup for a school or community performance. Study what the makeup designer suggests. Experiment with the type of makeup used. Learn the difference between stage makeup and what you put on during the day.

Volunteer to help a professional photographer. Study how light affects the appearance of people being photographed. Offer to apply makeup for studio portraits. Experiment with ways to make people look good under photo lights.

Research makeup classes offered for young people in your area. Spas and beauty salons often have workshops.

Keep pictures of the different looks you create and develop a picture gallery of your work.

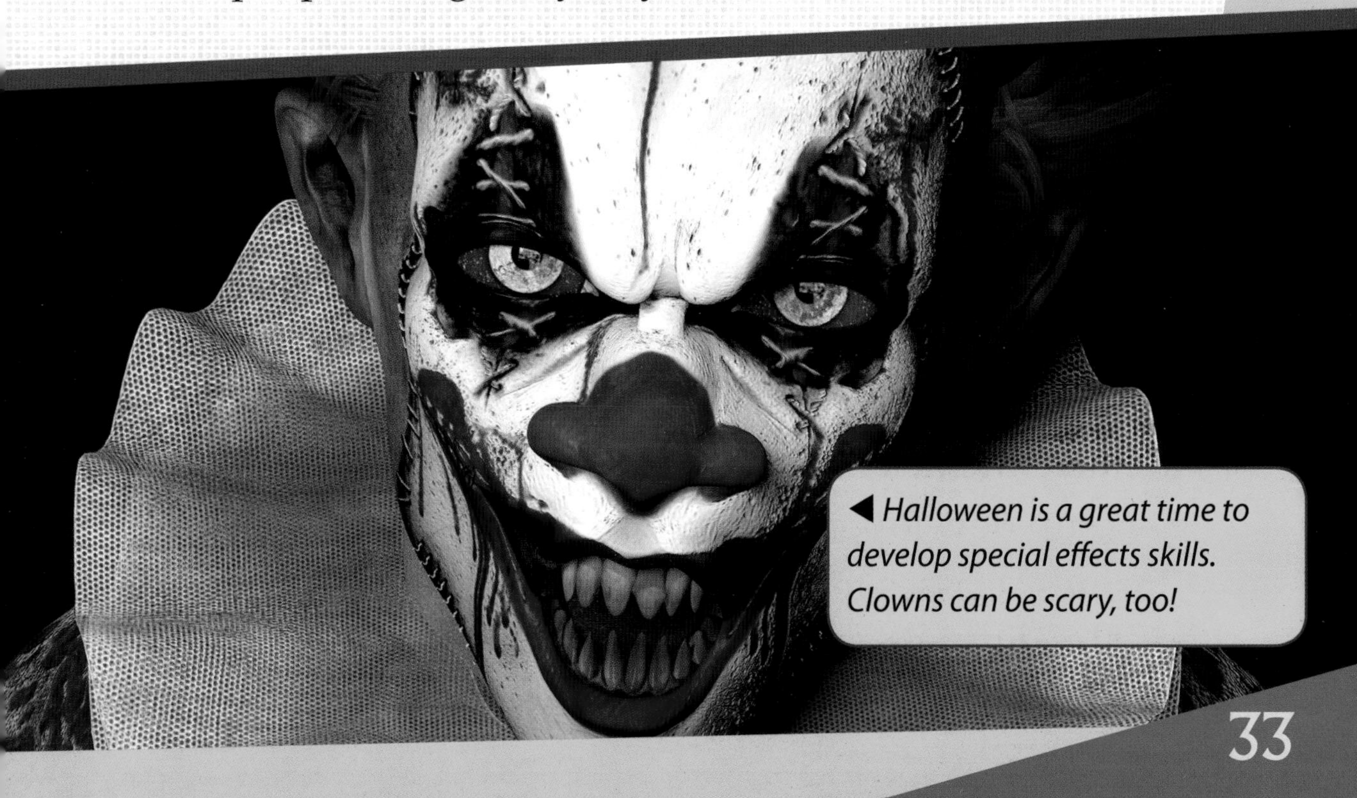

◀ *Halloween is a great time to develop special effects skills. Clowns can be scary, too!*

Education

▲ *Makeup artists need computer skills for researching looks of the past for inspiration.*

Most makeup artists finish high school and then take a special makeup course. Someone who loves applying makeup should search the Internet for schools that offer classes in makeup artistry.

High School

Many high school courses help future makeup artists.

- English and history classes teach research skills.
- Art classes provide information about how to use and blend colors.
- Health classes talk about the skin and how to take care of it.
- Some science classes focus on light and how it affects vision. This is useful for people interested in photographic makeup.
- Chemistry classes deal with compounds and how to make them. This provides background for makeup developers.
- Business classes teach public relations, marketing, and bookkeeping.

After High School

High school graduates can train as makeup artists at a number of different colleges. Check with your guidance counselor and research online to learn what courses are offered in your area.

Did You Know?

Bad teeth can be covered with tooth enamel or tooth covering. Good teeth can be made to look rotten using the same products.

Most successful makeup artists were formally trained and have advanced study certificates. This doesn't need to be a time-consuming process. Some programs can take as little as six months. Another option is cosmetology programs, which take 12 to 24 months to complete. **Certification** may be required for some jobs and states. To find out what's needed in a particular state, check the regulations.

▶ *This teen is doing the makeup for her high school's theater production.*

Famous Makeup Schools

There are many makeup schools throughout North America. Here are four that are well-known.

Cinema Makeup School

Cinema Makeup School in Los Angeles, California, offers diploma programs in Master Makeup, Film & TV Makeup, Professional Makeup, and High Fashion Makeup. The length of the program varies from 6 weeks to 18 weeks. Its classes give students hands-on experience and are taught by experienced makeup artists. The Cinema Makeup School is geared toward makeup artists who want to work in the entertainment field.

▼ *Students at Cinema Makeup School in Hollywood, California, can take a special effects makeup course.*

Douglas Education Center

This school near Pittsburgh, Pennsylvania, has a Special Make-Up Effects Program taught by Tom Savini, an award-winning special effects artist. The 16-month program includes courses in cosmetic makeup, character makeup, animatronics, mold making, and creature design.

Makeup Designory

Another great school is Makeup Designory, or MUD. They have campuses on both the West and East coasts of the United States and 10 studios throughout the world. The courses include hands-on work as well as demonstrations and lectures.

CMC Makeup School

CMC Makeup School has campuses in Dallas, Houston, Austin, and San Antonio, Texas. CMC Makeup School trains makeup artists for the beauty industry. It offers courses on glamour, high fashion, photography, and runway makeup.

▼ *Makeup school students learn all the skills they will need when working in fashion industry.*

Makeup Portfolio

▲ *Use your best work as the first photograph in your portfolio.*

Some states require that makeup artists be certified, while others don't. However, all makeup artists should have a portfolio. They should take pictures of their work starting as early as when they're in training.

What Goes In

Make sure that your portfolio book opens and lies flat so that several people can look at it at the same time.

Design a number of looks for your market. Make up a face chart for each look and include all of the details. You want to produce samples that show your style and passion, in addition to the skills you've mastered. It is always a good idea to experiment with unusual looks.

All photographs in the portfolio should be in focus and of good quality. Use your best work as the first photograph in your portfolio. If your work has been used for television or film, include a production still. It is also important to ask for testimonials from people you've worked with and include them in your portfolio.

Getting the Material

To get material for your portfolio, offer your services for free to professional photographers, models, and hairstylists. By working together, you can help each other. The photographer, model, or hairstylist may have suggestions for you. Adopt the ones you like. Get photos.

Post the portfolio on your own website, Tumblr, Pinterest, and other places.

Did You Know?

Ears are slightly lighter and redder in color than adjacent skin tones. Cover them with a base makeup that is two or three shades darker than the face to make them look normal in photos. Cover this base with a translucent face powder.

▼ *For a portfolio, take pictures of clients before and after their makeup is applied.*

Famous Makeup Artists

▲ Rick Baker has been working in the movie industry since the early 1970s.

Lon Chaney, Sr.

(April 1, 1883–August 26, 1930)

Lon Chaney, Sr. was the founding father of special effects makeup. He created special effects for acclaimed films, such as *The Hunchback of Notre Dame* (1923), *The Monster* (1925), and *The Phantom of the Opera* (1925). His work shaped the special effects industry. Many of his adoring fans refered to him as "the man of a thousand faces."

▲ Lon Chaney, Sr. was one of the most famous actors and makeup artists of the silent movie era.

Rick Baker

(born December 8, 1950)

Rick Baker is a highly-sought-after and world-famous makeup artist and special effects designer. He has achieved top honors in the special effects makeup artist industry, earning an astounding seven Academy Awards. He is best known for creating gorilla-type characters for epic movies, including the remakes of *King Kong* and *The Planet of the Apes*.

▲ *Bobbi Brown strives to empower women through optimizing their looks.*

Bobbi Brown

(born April 16, 1957)

Bobbi Brown is a well-known makeup artist and founder of Bobbi Brown Cosmetics. She began her career as a makeup artist in 1980 after moving to New York City. Her work stood out because she used milder colors than other makeup artists who at the time were using vibrant colors.

Sam Fine

(born November 12, 1969)

Sam Fine started his career at store makeup counters, where he learned how to use colors and shades to help women look their best. He was the first African-American spokesperson for Revlon and CoverGirl, and he launched his own line—Sam Fine for Fashion Fair—in 2013.

▲ *Sam Fine developed looks for African-American skin tones and wrote a book based on his work.*

Makeup in the Past

▲ *During the 1500s, people used makeup made from white lead.*

Early humans painted their faces and bodies to prepare for hunting, religious rituals, and battle. They made colors from charcoal, ground minerals, and plants.

Historic Makeup

Egyptians used **kohl** for eyeliner. Kohl is a black powder made from **lead**. Egyptians tinted their eyes and eyebrows with green from copper. They ground beetles to make a red powder for their lips and cheeks.

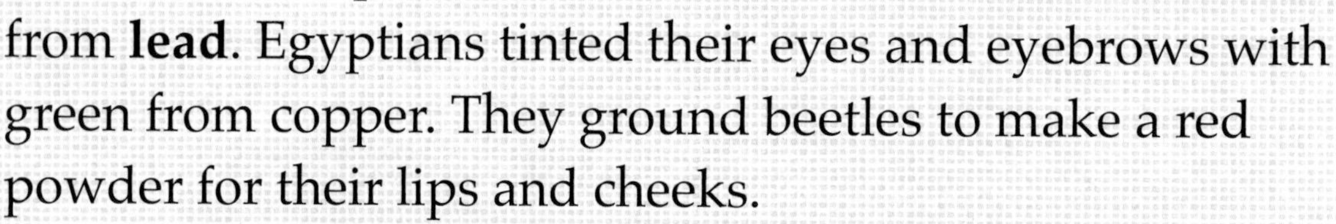

During the 1500s, Queen Elizabeth I popularized the use of white lead face paint. Burnt corks gave dark colors.

▼ *Egyptian paintings dating from 4000 BCE show both men and women wearing makeup.*

Modern Makeup

Once electric lights started being used in theaters, actors who wore white powder as stage makeup looked too pale. During the 1860s, a singer and chemistry student named Ludwig Leichner developed greasepaint using lard and other ingredients. With greasepaint, actors looked more natural. Greasepaint could be dyed, did not melt with perspiration, and lasted longer.

Did You Know?

Lead and arsenic were common ingredients in historic makeup, sometimes causing illness and death. At the time, no one knew about their harmful effects.

In 1914, Max Factor developed a flexible greasepaint that made actors look natural on film. In 1918, he developed face powder in a range of colors and later created pancake makeup. This makeup is applied with a sponge, covers up imperfections, and provides an even skin tone.

▼ *Each Native American tribe had its own designs for body paint.*

You Can Be a Makeup Artist

Do you still want to be a makeup artist? Check out the following characteristics. Which traits do you have? Which ones are you developing?

▲ *Watch demonstrations on YouTube and practice with your friends.*

I am

- ❒ artistic
- ❒ flexible
- ❒ punctual
- ❒ organized
- ❒ hardworking
- ❒ patient

I enjoy

- ❒ working with colors
- ❒ helping people look their best
- ❒ learning how actors and models achieve the effects they do

If you have or are developing these traits, you might make a great makeup artist.

▼ *If there's a theme park or historic site in your area, find out about any makeup jobs. Large sites often need professionals to do makeup. Offer to assist them!*

Set Your Goal

Decide what kind of makeup artist you want to be. Research the needed training either online or by talking to a guidance counselor. Find out:

- Which high school credits will be useful?
- Which schools offer the courses you want?
- What do you need to get into those schools?

▲ *Art lessons in color and balance and drawing can help develop skills needed to be a special effects makeup artist.*

Take Steps Now

Research local stores. Which ones have makeup counters? Apply for a job demonstrating and selling makeup. Observe the shoppers. Start to analyze their needs and make suggestions.

Keep notes about the looks you create. Write down the details of how you created any new colors.

Photograph what you do and upload the photos to Facebook, Tumblr, and MySpace. Get a Twitter account and network with makeup artists. Subscribe to the blogs of known makeup artists.

Glossary

airbrush an atomizer using compressed air to spray a liquid, such as paint, on a surface

bald cap a wig-like cap to create the appearance of a bald head

certification official approval to do something professionally or legally

character a person represented in a play, film, story, etc.

client a person who pays for a service

concealer a type of makeup that is used to hide blemishes

dermatologist a doctor who specializes in diseases of the skin

enhance to improve something

kohl eyeliner that is deeply black in color, no longer made from lead

latex a white fluid produced by certain plants, used for making rubber

lead a toxic chemical

palette a range of colors used for a particular project

plaster of Paris a white powdery, slightly hydrated calcium sulfate used chiefly for casts and molds in the form of a quick-setting paste

plastic surgeon a doctor who performs surgery to improve or repair a person's appearance

primer a makeup product (cream, gel, or liquid) used before applying a makeup foundation; it preps the skin by smoothing out pores and fine lines

prosthetics artificial devices used to replace or augment a part of the body

silicone rubber rubber noted for its flexibility, resilience, and strength

spirit gum a solution used especially for attaching false hair to the skin

translucent not completely clear or transparent, but clear enough to allow light to pass through

For More Information

Books

Academy of Freelance Makeup. *Makeup Is Art: Professional Techniques for Creating Original Looks*. London: Carlton Books, 2011.

Craig, Jonathan. *Special Effects Make-up Artist: The Coolest Jobs on the Planet*. London: Raintree, 2013.

Horn, Geoffrey M. *Movie Makeup, Costumes, and Sets (Making Movies)*. New York, NY: Gareth Stevens Publishing, 2006.

Websites

The Hair & Makeup Artist Network (HMAN)
www.hmartistsnetwork.com/about-the-network
Provides career support for freelance makeup artists.

International Makeup Association (IMA)
www.ima-makeup.com/about.htm
Provides international qualifications in the field.

Vancouver Film School (VFS)
www.vfs.edu/programs/makeup#play_tertiary_video
Get a taste of the what students learn during a makeup course.

Index